Contents

GW00367367

Group focus

It'll help with the running of *Parentalk – The Primary Years*, and make it more enjoyable, if we can stick to a few ways of working together:

- Always be on time
- Remember that no one expects you always to have something to say
- As a general rule, let everyone have a first word before you have your second!
- Don't talk about things discussed during *Parentalk* with others outside the group
- Don't say, "If I were you …!"

- Encourage others in the group. We need each other
- If you have concerns about anything that takes place or anything that you hear, talk to the group leader first before taking any other action
- Be kind to yourself. The very fact that you're doing the course says you care about being an even better parent

Session 1:

IT'S NOT JUST ME

When we become parents, our lives change forever.

Unfortunately, children don't come with instruction manuals, and most of us feel inadequate at times. Sometimes we can feel as though we're making it all up as we go along! It's important to realise that there is no such thing as a perfect parent, but we can all be good parents.

Sharing our struggles and failures can actually help us to realise that it's not 'just me' facing those particular challenges. If we only tell others our 'best bits' it paints a false picture of what family life is really like.

Remember...

- As parents, we are all in the same boat!

- Parenting plays havoc with your emotions

- Parenting is fun as well as challenging at times

- Accept yourself; it's not possible to be the perfect parent

- Don't forget the joys of parenting

Does having children make life more stressful?

Spotlight on 'My story'

Being a mum or dad of young children can be hard work. Sometimes it can feel as though other people are looking over our shoulders and making judgements on our parenting.

Most parents feel inadequate and guilty at times. That's why one mum said: "I feel guilty all the time, I feel guilty when I drop them off and I feel guilty when I pick them up. I feel guilty about what they eat, what they don't eat, what they might eat! I'm starting to think that guilt comes attached to the placenta."

Don't be tempted to compare yourself with other parents or to compare your children with other people's children.

Life completely changes when you become a parent. Often we can be surprised by how much it affects our emotions. We might feel a loss of identity because the interests and activities that made us who we were as an individual or a couple have now taken a back seat or perhaps disappeared altogether. Our new role in life as a mum or dad can also feel very scary and knock our confidence.

There are always pressures for us as parents whether we work full-time, part-time or stay at home.

Diane's top tip

"Get rid of the mask, and be honest with one another."

Final thoughts

If we want to be the best parents we can be, it's important to look after ourselves as well as our children. Try to build in some 'me' time.

Perhaps we could:

- Read a book
- Have a bath – with the door shut!
- Go for a run
- Meet a friend for a drink
- Spend some time with our partner without the children present

What's *the* one thing you want to remember from this session?

Session 2:
LOVE THEM AND LET THEM KNOW

All human beings have a need for love and security, and our children look to us, as their mums and dads, to provide this. Every child is different – they have different personalities and respond to things in different ways, so it's important that we show love to them in a way they personally understand.

What's the best way to show a child that you love them?

Remember...

- All children are different
- Our children need to know that they are loved for who they are, not for what they achieve
- We all have an 'emotional tank' that needs topping up

Spotlight on 'My story'

Our children are all different, and it can sometimes be difficult to know how to respond to them individually.

Love languages

In his book *The 5 Love Languages*®, Dr Gary Chapman suggests that there are five ways in which people commonly express love*. This is through words, gifts, actions, time or touch. These 'love languages' help us to understand how to show our children love in the way that they best understand.

Words

This isn't just about telling our children that we love them – although that's important. It's about praising and encouraging them too. If words are a child's love language, put-downs and unkind comments will have a greater negative impact on them.

Gifts

The value of the gift doesn't necessarily matter; it's the thought and effort behind it that is as important as the gift itself. If gifts are a child's love language, a thoughtlessly chosen present is likely to make them feel hurt or unappreciated.

Touch

Holding hands with our three-year-old, giving their older sister a hug, putting a hand on the shoulder or giving a pat on the back to our 'almost' teenager will be a real emotional connection for them. If a child's love language is touch, they may feel hurt or neglected if we pull away when they try to hug us.

Time

Uninterrupted, quality time with mum or dad – whether it's little and often or a large chunk – will make a world of difference. It won't necessarily matter if a day out gets ruined by the rain. What matters is the time spent with us. If time is a child's love language, it is likely to be particularly frustrating for them if they don't have our undivided attention when we are together.

Actions

Helping with homework, showing our child how to make pizza, or picking them up when they fall off their bike all show love in action. If actions are a child's love language, they may feel especially hurt by laziness or by commitments that are broken by us or other family members.

Our children need all these expressions of love particularly when they are still young. However, as they get older, we may find that one or two of these love languages are especially important for them. Once we learn to recognise our child's love language, we can use it to show them love in a way that they really understand and respond to.

*www.5lovelanguages.com

For children to really thrive, they need to know that they are loveable, that they are valued, and that they are safe.

Perhaps we could:

- Catch them doing something right
- Praise them for something they've done well at school
- Put a note in their lunch box to encourage them
- Say "I love it when you .... (fill in the blank)"
- Praise them for how they behaved in a social situation
- Say something nice about them to another adult when they're in earshot

Final thoughts

Children love to be congratulated and encouraged. Look for opportunities to praise them for their individual gifts and talents.

What's *the* one thing you want to remember from this session?

Session 3:

Communication is an important part of family life and includes listening as well as talking to our children.

Words are powerful. They can teach, give encouragement, and express love and forgiveness, but they also have the potential to hurt and damage. Let's make what we say to our children count for good and tune in to what they're saying.

Why do you think it's important for parents to talk to and listen to their children?

Remember...

- We can help our children feel valued by listening to them and giving them our full attention

- Children can find it hard to express themselves. Sometimes we need to listen to the feelings behind the words

- Active listening includes stopping what we are doing, physically getting down to their level, looking them in the face, giving them eye contact and being patient.

Spotlight on 'My story'

It can be so easy to be distracted when our children try to talk to us, and sometimes it can be hard to understand their seemingly irrational fears.

When we can, we need to try to be 'available' for our children. This isn't the same as just being physically present. Being available means giving our children our full attention and not being distracted by other things.

Understanding that our children's fears are real, however irrational they may seem, can really help us to understand their world better.

Children sometimes struggle to express their feelings, but we can help them by showing how it's done ourselves – for example, "Mummy is feeling a bit sad at the moment".

Children don't always want pick the most convenient time for a conversation; often it seems to be when we're at our busiest. As much as possible, try to be ready to listen when they want to talk, and take up any opportunities to communicate that spontaneously arise.

Creating the right environment can really help family communication – for example, at meals times or on car journeys.

Mark's top tip

"Sometimes we need to put away all distractions and give our children our full attention. And they need to know that they have our full attention."

Final thoughts

We need to be intentional about talking with our children. Plan to spend time with them individually, and create opportunities for good communication.

Perhaps we could:

- Go out for breakfast together
- Go for a walk
- Do a craft activity together
- Play a game or do a jigsaw puzzle
- Do a job together – for example, gardening, cooking or DIY

What's *the* one thing you want to remember from this session?

Session 4:

BOUNDARIES AND BATTLES

Children's behaviour can be something of a battleground.

It is important that our expectations are fair, that our children understand them, and that we are clear and consistent about what happens when a boundary is crossed. If we share parental responsibilities, we need to ensure that we work together as a team and that we don't undermine each other if we have different approaches to discipline.

> Why do you think that children need boundaries?

Spotlight on 'My story'

Children frequently test the boundaries, often just to see what reaction they will get from us. Often one of the difficulties in parenting is being consistent in the way we respond.

We need to put boundaries in place for our children. As well as being important for creating a peaceful family life, boundaries are essential because they give our children security, teach them self-control, and help them understand that there are consequences for their actions.

Boundaries need to be fair, clearly communicated, and understood by both us and our children. We also need to be consistent in the way we respond to them.

Before jumping to conclusions, sometimes we need to look behind seemingly 'naughty' behaviour to see if there is anything else going on. It could be that our children are tired or hungry and are not just misbehaving.

The ways people behave as parents (known as parenting styles) usually fall into three types:

Authoritarian

"Do as you are told and don't argue."

Parents have strict ideas about discipline and behaviour and are not open to discussion. They tend to be bossy and controlling. Children of authoritarian parents may do what they're told – but out of fear, or they may end up being rebellious and defiant.

Permissive

"Do whatever you want."

Parents have very relaxed ideas about behaviour and discipline and just want to be friends with their children. They tend to find it difficult to lay down boundaries and may not see the need. Children of permissive parents may end up feeling like their parents don't care or don't love them.

Assertive

"You can do that if…"
"You can't do that because…"

Parents have ideas about behaviour and discipline that they are willing to explain and discuss with their children. They give appropriate freedom within limits. Children of assertive parents feel safe, secure and more confident.

Sometimes we need to be flexible and go back to our children when we've got things wrong. We also need to be willing to apologise to them when necessary and show them that we can admit our own mistakes.

We need to be willing to follow through on consequences, even if it makes us unpopular.

Kunle's top tip

"Be consistent; say what you mean and mean what you say."

Final thoughts

- Whatever style of parenting we were brought up with, we can decide for ourselves what kind of parent we want to be. Aim to be an assertive parent – firm but fair

- Remember that it's always more effective when we can take a united approach to discipline with our child's other parent

What's *the* one thing you want to remember from this session?

Session 5:
PARENTING WITH ELASTIC

As parents we are involved in the process of helping our children become independent.

It's natural, though, to sometimes find it hard to let them go as our instinct is to want to protect them. 'Parenting with elastic' is about encouraging our children towards independence, helping them learn life skills, and enabling them to make good choices. Somehow we have to find the right balance between keeping them safe, without over-protecting them.

Remember...

- As parents, we're hardwired to want to protect our children

- If we want to give our children responsibility, we need to learn to let them go bit by bit

- Passing on our values to our children will help them to make good choices in the future

How much freedom should parents give their children?

Spotlight on 'My story'

At each stage of a child's life we have to learn to 'let go' a little, whether it's when they learn to walk, when they start school, or when they go to the shops on their own for the first time. Every one of these new phases may be difficult for us, but we do need to allow them to take risks and show that we trust them.

We can sometimes find being a parent harder as our children get older because we still love them as much as ever, but we have less control of them. Our roles as parents move from control, to care, to counsel.

We don't do our children any favours if we always come to their rescue; sometimes they need to learn from their mistakes.

We are the biggest influence in our children's lives; we can show our children our values and how we want them to behave by demonstrating it ourselves.

We want our children to make wise choices about life in a world of unlimited choices. We can help to equip them when they are still young by giving them the opportunity to make decisions about the little things – for example, about what they wear, eat or play with.

Diane's top tip

"If you want your children to pick up your values for themselves, the best thing that you can do is model them."

Final thoughts

Values are more often caught than taught. What are the values that are important to you and your family?

They could be:

- Being generous to other people
- Making the most of every opportunity
- Honesty
- Everyone helping each other out
- Looking after the environment

What's *the* one thing you want to remember from this session?

Session 6:

CREATING A SENSE OF BELONGING

Creating strong family memories with our children through fun, laughter and traditions is important.

If we have few happy memories from our own childhood, this may be a painful subject for us as we think about what might have been. Although we can't go back to change the past, it is important to recognise that we can still help to build positive memories with our own children.

What fun things do you like to do as a family?

Spotlight on 'My story'

Sometimes we need to set time aside to have fun as a family. We can start now to create new memories together.

Shared memories are like 'relationship glue' for families. Each time we recall and laugh about them, they strengthen the bond between us.

Family traditions help to give children roots, create a sense of belonging, and give individual family members the sense of being part of a 'team'.

It's good to do spontaneous, fun things sometimes and to be willing to laugh at ourselves, even if it means we might feel silly.

Whatever our previous experience of family life, whether it was good or bad, we have the opportunity to make our own memories with our children. We can take the best of what we've done in the past and create new traditions together as a family.

Traditions often come about simply by chance; something that happened once that everyone enjoyed – at Christmas, for example – can quickly become a family custom. They don't need to be sophisticated or expensive – they might well something very simple that our children enjoy doing.

Final thoughts

What new memories can we create?

Perhaps we could:

- Have a family film night with home-made popcorn
- Go for a 'nature walk' in the dark with torches
- Create a 'restaurant' at home, including designing a menu and getting the children to help out with the cooking
- Take silly photos of one another and give a prize for the silliest
- Go camping – put a tent up in the garden and spend the night sleeping under canvas

Mark's top tip

"Find something that works for your family, and repeat it time and time again."

What's *the* one thing you want to remember from this session?

Thank you

We hope you've enjoyed *Parentalk – The Primary Years*.

If you found this course helpful, you may want to explore some of the topics in a little more depth by going on one of our popular *Time Out for Parents* courses. To find out more, visit: www.careforthefamily.org.uk/courses.

If you would like further help in your parenting, you can find a list of parent support organisations on our website at www.careforthefamily.org.uk/parenting.

Care for the Family has a range of resources for parents including books, events, DVDs, articles and newsletters. We also provide support for couples and for those who have been bereaved.

We'd love to hear what you thought of *Parentalk – The Primary Years*, you can let us know by giving feedback at www.surveymonkey.com/s/parentalk. This will only take about 5 minutes and will help us to make sure that the course remains a useful resource for all parents.

For more information:
- 029 2081 0800
- www.careforthefamily.org.uk
- www.facebook.com/careforthefamily
- www.twitter.com/Care4theFamily

About Care for the Family

Care for the Family is a registered charity and has been working to strengthen family life since 1988. Our aim is to promote strong family relationships and to help those who face family difficulties. Working throughout the UK and the Isle of Man, we provide parenting, relationship and bereavement support through our events, resources, courses, training and volunteer networks. Our work is motivated by Christian compassion, and our resources and support are available to everyone, of any faith or none.

Welcome to *Parentalk – The Primary Years*

Being a parent is one of life's greatest joys, but it is also one of its biggest challenges.

There's hardly a mum or dad on the face of the earth who, at times, is not overawed by the task of parenting. At Care for the Family we know that mums and dads can feel under tremendous pressure to be the 'perfect parent', and because of this they can often end up feeling guilty. That's why we've created *Parentalk*.

Parentalk – The Primay Years is a DVD-based resource for small groups which covers topics that affect every family with children in the early years through to the early teens. As you go through each session you will be able to talk to other parents in your group about the day-to-day challenges that you face, as well as the things that are going well.

This little booklet is yours to keep. You may want to jot down ideas of things you'd like to try at home or take some notes during the sessions to remind you of what you've talked about.

Thank you for taking the time to do *Parentalk – The Primary Years*. We hope you'll discover that you're not on your own in some of the challenges that you face – other parents are in the same boat! And we hope you'll realise that you're *already* a fantastic mum or dad. Most of all, we hope you'll be reminded that while being a parent has its fair share of difficulties at times, it is also one of the greatest jobs in the world!

Rob Parsons

Rob Parsons OBE
Founder and Chairman of Care for the Family

Parentalk

THE PRIMARY YEARS